Side Show

T0163501

SIDE SHOW   *poems*

CATHERINE FRENCH

UNIVERSITY OF NEVADA PRESS / RENO & LAS VEGAS

This project is supported by funding from the National Endowment for the Arts

Western Literature Series

University of Nevada Press, Reno, Nevada 89557 USA

Copyright © 1988, 1989, 1990, 1991, 1992, 1993, 1994, 1996, 1998, 2002 by Catherine French

All rights reserved

Manufactured in the United States of America

Design by Carrie House

Library of Congress Cataloging-in-Publication Data

French, Catherine, 1961–

Side show : poems / Catherine French.

p. cm. — (Western literature series)

ISBN 0-87417-512-7 (pbk. : alk. paper)

I. Title. II. Series.

PS3606.R46 S53 2002

811'.6—dc21 2002000644

The paper used in this book meets the requirements of American National Standard for Information Sciences—Permanence of Paper for Printed Library Materials, ANSI Z39.48-1984. Binding materials were selected for strength and durability.

FIRST PRINTING

11 10 09 08 07 06 05 04 03 02

5 4 3 2 1

For Gary Short

Contents

PRESTO CHANGE-O!

Acknowledgments

Grateful acknowledgement is made to the editors of the following journals in which versions of these poems first appeared: *Bakunin* for "Fortunetelling Fish" (1991); *Gettysburg Review* for "The Irresistible," "October," and "Straw Man" (1996); *The Iowa Review* for "Bent July Landscape" (1990); *Mankato Poetry Review* for "Duck Pickers," "The Forties," "Lantern," and "Opossum" (1988); *Nation* for "Alphabet" (1992); *Dry Heat* and *Poetry Flash* for "The Woman Who Fell from the Observation Deck of the Empire State Building Confesses" (1990); *Poetry Northwest* for "At the Edge of a Continent, Releasing the Dreams" and "Huntington's Disease" (1989); *Quarterly West* for "One Day in the Whale" (1994); *River City* for "Gogol, Toward St. Petersburg" and "Unmaking the Horse" (1989); *Suisun Valley Review* for "Afterlife" (1998).

Some poems in this manuscript were included in the chapbook *Boy with Viola and Other Poems,* published by Dry Heat Press, Phoenix, Arizona, 1995.

I want to thank the San Francisco Foundation for the James D. Phelan Literary Award. I also extend my deepest thanks to the following people who provided a vital mix of encouragement, humor, and sharpness during the writing of this book: Lisa Dominguez Abraham, Steve Bryant, Melissa Dubose, David Fritz, Anne French, Chris French, Rene Guillory, Denise Lichtig, Amy Makarchuk, Regina Marler, Mimi and Burnett Miller, Gary Short, Terrie Sultan, Zita and Jon Weil.

MUMBO JUMBO

Alphabet

The truth is I dreaded each wide letter
and by extension the aging yellow-white pages
with the standard letter-bearers—apple, zebra,
xylophone, coat. These physical counterparts
were secret code I would never crack—the yak
a mat of hair headed for slaughter
or a tundra isolation; the ball, untouched
in a sunless backyard, round and red and unattainable;
the blue dress on a white hanger,
freed from sticky flesh. I knew
how they failed in that attempt to join
the physical and abstract, how each sound
fell short of the world. But fear gives way
to routine, and routine yields up
its indirection, that sing-song
also a simple path away
until what remains is as unnoticeable
and profound as mother's heartbeat and blood flow,
those first unviewed x's a rhythm beat
into soft flesh as certainly as large black letters
embed into page—the traffic washing by at night,
the crickets speaking like Martians, the wind
pushing dried leaves across cement in bursts.
When I close the book, they hang before me
like dizzying hummingbirds, my own thought
refusing to settle or still to a hard line
and unable to return to full quiet.

Straw Man

He bumps up blind between my shoulders,
having followed too close. The crude ink eyes
appear to see, and the crayoned-on mouth
is perched to speak. But his quiet
strings invisibly between us.

Lying in bed at night with him
beside me, I listen to the rustle
of my breath and his inert complicity.
We rise in tandem, one of his limp arms
resting on my shoulder. I lead him
like this in obligation.

When he first arrived no one
was more surprised than I to find him
there beside me. Shapeless,
gesturing toward the more real.
And even I, an escape artist, couldn't
slip him. His vagueness oddly persisted,

an airy yellow middle held near
my own in a kind of game
without motive. I suppose outrage
was predictable, as it always is
when what we have sent out returns.

But humor, too. Spirit sifting through
the straw for a comfortable bed.
A joke, you see. The first and continuing joke.
A sack of flour, a bag of sugar.
Some things make you remember more than others
where you stand and who stands with you,
grinning, waiting quietly for you to notice.

Lyric with Disorderly Tendencies

The garlic on my fingertips
returns the hours—oil in a pan,
cut yellow pepper, wine poured
and the wind through chimes,
each note the collision of bone,
a happy sound.

The grapevine over trellis
and over the chimes
is curling, lush.
If we could choose
we'd rather be those bushes—
the bees walking through us.

The hay bales loosened out of symmetry
make a stair and lookout for night.
We want open heaven,
the cut moon and blue field
to be enough.
Instead, we are caught
like the wasp on the kitchen table
this morning, its husk coiled
in a dish-towel thread.

The immature grapes,
so obviously unready, will turn
from their sour tight circles
and swell to sweetness.
They've just arrived.
They've yet to voice their demands
or fall from them.

Huntington's Disease

If you can stand the pressure
of all that water, the distance down
you have to travel, and the blindness
you must swim into not knowing
if it is place or death or both,
you win the chance to see life
lived in darkness. The lingcod
which eats its own, thick
wolf-eels staring blindly
like your disconsolate grandfather,
the fierce sunflower starfish prying
bodies apart with its inching arms
(the hand exaggerated and cut off from the head),
creatures sulking in the cracks,
waiting for death, thinking about it,
thinking about the bad neighborhood they're in.
And if you swim out, back up
to light and warmth, rays bent toward you,
you'll realize you're a prisoner forever.
It might take a month, maybe years
for everything to go dark, for
the cracks to open,
but the wolf-eel and lingcod, mouths open,
will swim slowly through you
and make your hands shake.

The Forties

Because of the war, we had the beaches
at Half Moon Bay when the sun begins to slide
out of the crest of noon, the light dancing off
the water like a Ginger Rogers dress.
We were eleven—me, Spud, Joe and Willie—
didn't know what we had, thought
the beaches were an okay place to hang out
and eat crab, 75 cents, a dollar, with sourdough.
You just had to be downwind of the elephant seals
the fishermen shot for poaching from their nets.
They'd wash up on shore and soak the sand dark,
grounded in their massive frames.
Dared, we'd stick our fingers in the dry wrinkles,
pry a huge clamped mouth to measure
the teeth with our thumbs and finally
climb on, riding the mammoth death.

A Light Ash Before Them

In God's dry stomach
faith is marble
and love with the statues
unable to be roused.
The statues would agree
there are breaks
which preclude return.
The body, say, coming to a place—
not the simple walk
from here to here
but standing still as the old life
collapses like straw
in a strong wind and the sun goes down
weak and white. You stare
at the church ceiling,
at the neat squares. Counting them
is a way to pass the time
when you might otherwise behave badly.
One, two. So precise.
Three, four, a monopoly of shape,
like the human form.
Which lies down in fever.
Which lights the candles
and can't sleep.
Perfume doesn't quite mask tallow,
and the mind travels
to a memory of death,
the animal's spirit
stepping around its body
as a man stepped around a manhole
on the street. Hundreds
of fingers counting beads, words

become a murmur. Down the pew,
a boy fiddles with a coat clasp.
With his tongue, he lifts
and lowers the metal clasp
until he slips, and his tongue is hit hard.
His change in expression is accomplished
in silence. You watch the rows
of red glass cupping the votives, their lights
thrown by motion or invisible presence.
Some women will come in
and sit for a long time in silence,
the way well water settles slowly
after something is dropped in it.
You try to catch the statues
watching you and think you know
all about them—How they must love
the flowers drying at their feet
and our blur,
a light ash before them.

Temporary Expressions Leave Permanent Traces

A meadowlark breaks from an almond tree
and my brother shoots it,
the red and white stripes
of his shirt a kind of flag. He's a boy
and knows nothing yet
but shame at killing a songbird.

There's a horse in a paddock by the tree, a bathtub
for the horse's water,
algae on the bottom
like the fur of a struck piano key.
It's summer. We wade through
dry fields, then pick off the thistles
and burrs that catch in our clothes,
flick them back to the ground.

He wants to retrieve the second
the horse flinched,
her skin shivering
then calming, like water.
But her thick bones
still hold the sound.

In the afternoon, my sister
and I flood the garden,
water spilling through the chicken yard.
Regret prickles like the splintering
barn at our backs.

The bird,
the horse,
the water,
those chickens.
It's July and we sway in the heat.

By night,
mistakes snare in my skin. As I sleep
in the circle of yellow hills,
they crack open
and their deeper life begins.

Opossum

The flooded river forced it up that night,
wedged it between the shed and the house.
Its pinkened cataracts the first we knew.
Then the hiss swelled in it, pitching to a rasp.
When we stretched the hose,
sprayed to the back, intent,
it shuffled out,
blinking in light, dripping into the dog crate.

We kept it a day, watched it
shift the small hands on the thin bars.
It focused inward unless we moved too near;
then teeth glowed, crescent,
as it grinned.

Returned to the river, the door open,
it lurked a moment, stunned.
Then a silver ripple, then gone.

Harvest

There was a freedom—Parents out of town
and pumpkins stashed in the cellar,
six heads glowing like sin. The boys couldn't wait
and we broke into them two weeks early, reveling
in the rich, slightly fecal-smelling hollows, like a band
of loose pigs. The carving took so little time
and there they were, grinning—our beautiful
orange faces, perfect, crooked and lit.
Even the classroom's torpor, the spoil of sweat
that unfolded like clockwork with thickets
of problems, couldn't slow the quick of that month.
Those same yellows and reds had taken over the world,
dripping from trees and rising every day
sharp and burning. We raced through color,
didn't even notice the first stipple of spore until wider
streaks of black and brown had colonized the cavities
and white began to take the heads. My oldest brother
knew to wrap his in foil and let us buy shares for a quarter
in his more slowly devoured lantern, as ours puckered
and softened, mold feathering inside, then through
the eyes and teeth. I monitored the spoil, amazed.
That love couldn't hold them there, that each fresh notion
moldered into collapse, a slick layer for what came next.
That those lovely jagged faces withered and caved in.
It wasn't my first taste of change, but one that stung—
that shocking resonance of harvest hitting
the tongue and current rippling out,
leaving me awake, numb.

Live Burlesque

From my window, I see a fight,
the man chasing his beloved
to her car. He shoves
his face close to hers
chanting you whore, you slut,
until she flees.
Their lovemaking
isn't what it used to be.

When she drives out of range,
I have to imagine the rest.
I fail her too. We all need it
up close and in the face
before understanding breaks
like the clouds above me
about to drop their weight.
I could eat this before-rain feel
all my life—It's the scent of rescue.

When it finally does fall,
the streets clear.
Residual oils spiral open
and the smell of gasoline,
lush and volatile,
graces the air.

Elvis Impersonator

Heavy-lidded narcosis
is a good beginning,
mouth a bit off,
but the snarl will camouflage it.
Your hair should be shoe-polish black,
oiled, but sharp like a 20-year-old's.

Olive shadows should crush
about the eyes,
your pout must deny
the malignant universe.
Be buoyant,
light as a cat,
spill charm and nonchalance.

Now, register catastrophe
(Mama's dead).
Pile it on through the years,
whatever will hide you.
Here, it's easiest
to be a cliché. Still,
there's enough adoration
with the scorn. The women
will fight for your scarves
and sleep with them.

Your sunglasses
need to be the right degree
of retro. So does your world view.
It's the hardest time,

that pause
before celebrity takes you apart.

It's a relief finally
to curl up
and let the thing devour you
until it's finally full.
Then you'll leave yourself
lying in state, anonymous again.
But stop and look
before you're gone
at that long line
snaking through Graceland.

At the Edge of a Continent, Releasing the Dreams

They fall in slow motion, all of them,
from the exact moment he lets go
to when they hit
the bottom of the cliff.
Most break: the eggs,
China cups and occasional chair.
But with some he can't tell.
They lie still and then wash away.
The chicken, for instance, or the cat.
The sheets. And there was the milk,
absorbed by sand.
So those are the ones
that come back, bringing the sea
with them. He collapses under the weight
halfway through night, gulping air,
the muscles of his arms and calves
knotted against it.
Today, he drops a grapefruit
which splits on a rock before landing,
an opened eye. It is late, the light lifting,
and the tide comes for the fruit.
He watches the water dislodge it,
a pale yellow planet eased out of gravity,
salt washing through.

The Death of Birds

In Virginia City you can see six mountain ranges
from one porch. Basin and range,
basin and range, the land repeating itself
as in breathing. You have to watch
to realize the small differences in region.
Know which places contain the discolored
water pockets of the bombing range,
which birds inhabit Smith Valley. Or notice how
they've diminished, the birds, over the years,
how they don't all come back. The loss
is obscure, like the path of light on a given day,
because some do return, because they disappear
en route, dropping in ocean, a narrow slip
through surface, or in the stripped fields
where they dry to feather and bone.
They've given back their names—vireo,
thrush, wren, solitaire—given back flight
for paling flats of dust. But there,
in another country, you can only notice
the landscape's small turnings,
its full form concealed,
like your own death.

HOCUS POCUS

The Irresistible

Each time it is the same:
the bear catches the scent
and begins to run after the woman.
The pounding travels up her legs
as he draws near, and a low rumble
from his throat follows like sin.

Fear's thin ethanol
is irresistible, like carrion,
and the bear lumbers after
the good fortune. He can almost taste
the warm folded viscera
that will evaporate on the tongue.
Sweetness never lasts.
With his first glimpse,
his pupils snap open
like rosebuds in the light.

It's best if she doesn't run,
but she can't resist, and her fleeing
is hardly the work of an amateur.
Her shelter (in the layers
of tradition, the ramparts of order)
is temporary. The bear will
don the manners needed and the clothes
that grant entrance to the large house —
then the lit back rooms
of the library. He knows
what enticements will pull her

out to the steps for a word
to be whispered in her ear.

He stands on the porch
in his collars and gloves
as she stands behind the thick door
and listens to his breathing,
one hand resting on the doorknob.

October

I forget how he has come
to lounge on my couch, massaging his arm
that aches in the rising cold
near the line where it broke years ago.
His silence addresses the browns,
the yellows ascending in my skin.

His scent—half-smoke, half-earth—
effortlessly takes the room.
He draws to the ripening, drinking again.
Carrion, my sweet carrion,
he tells me with his eyes.

When he lifts one hand to my neck,
it isn't a chill, but the crack
of igniting dryness,
then a soft ash powders his fingertips.
He is telling me he doesn't know
the precise way to our imminent rise
when the beetle slips from his tongue
and chirrs like a wound-up toy
to my arm. Its wings fold like pages
of a letter skimmed and put away.
The legs scrape and hook as it climbs
up to my shoulder, a lozenge
making a deliberate path to my mouth.
It will collect the bead of devotion
then burrow in to feed.

Tendrils of lavender smoke drift
from the man on the couch, hibernating

until the beetle crawls across
the soft doorway of lip.

Then we will live.
Then we will dance into our death
and past it.

Molotov Cocktail

Its beginning was hardly auspicious—
the crash through window,
gasoline searing the air, seeing
the thing was lit.
But I didn't anticipate full incineration.
Best then to watch it transpire, progress
through its movements like serious art
and become a believer.
The slow way it builds from zero
to an inferno. Flame
sits in a chair, wraps around the legs,
then rests on the table and begins
to eat the polished surface.

It takes the room like a horse running.
And I can only watch it go, all
I'd gathered to shore up against the cold.
The furniture hisses and snaps
as it reduces to skeleton.
Hangings scorch, then flake off the walls
and, presto, the house has shed its skin.
I must have been high hazard, and now fire
climbs the stairs and rushes through
the doorways as though whatever lived there
finally after years stopped holding
its breath. Room after room
spins into orange blossom
and all the windows burst open.

Come morning, as I tiptoe through ash
and pick through the black filigree
for anything to save,

I'm sure loss will settle in my cells
with the torched smell.
Metaphors of renewal will fail
as I acquaint with blank ruin.
But for now I bask in sumptuous burn
and know, miles away,
what plays behind his cool eyes:
the bottle's lit neck just beginning to flare,
the throw, then brightness
and his gasp at the burst star.

Flock of Swifts

It is an outpouring like one of the plagues.
During the rainstorm, they wash like water
into the house, down the chimney, then into the front room
before they catch against the chain curtain
and cram the fireplace.

A rush of dust and ash, then the sound
of an earthquake. Except
it was the sky falling.
Not expected, but there's no avoiding
a flock of swifts in the house.

They hang like folded cloth in the mesh.
They hang in mute submission, the ash-gray breasts
pressing through grill, all the eyes blinking.
Not a note, just choked silence.

Their grand gesture is followed
by painful extrication. All the tiny feet
are carefully disengaged from metal chain.
Beating hearts and wings cupped
in the hand as group madness
is cured one by one. A mess, a wonder—
how the spirit freaks
and dives down deep,
finds the new world.

The Thief of Baghdad

The king was stupid, see, and became a blind beggar
to atone for his sins to the people. And Sabu was Abu—
get it?—and became a dog, so he didn't have to act
in those scenes. The dog did. Another king
wouldn't let go of the flying horse's head,
mechanical but miraculous. And Jaffar wore black,
of course, even around his eyes, and conjured
a lot of very neat animation for such a bad guy.

But that's not the point.
The only point of the whole movie is the genie.
The genie's out of the bottle
and he's enormous, much larger than King Kong.
He's enormous and he's laughing, and he's very angry
at having been kept in that damn bottle for so long,
and he's looking down at Sabu (or Abu) and that's it,
that's the moment in the celluloid roll,
but it's a big moment. And only one white-faced elephant
the whole movie. Poor Sabu, poor elephant boy.

Out of the Blue

The first man was an island.
The second, he was an island.
And the third also was an island.
It is clearly a chain;
They will all be islands.

He said . . . well, he didn't say.

And clarity threads up
Like a mob of blackbirds
Climbing the branches of a fir
Until the flock
Forces itself from the tree.

Out of quiet spills meaning,
Its tiny threads everywhere—
yellow, green, blue thread.

I can see the shapes
Truth assumes—island, bird, man.
And I shake each one
for one hum or thrush into my ear.
And they only crouch in my hands,
closed.

Such austere land
Rises out of the blue,
And the sky coolly looms above
As I sweat pearls.

Magdalen

I stumble through their disbelief—
that scold—and watch myself
consider them: the apostles
restless and circling. In its shock
the mind gropes over what it knows.

His opened tomb, as if I stood
in my own heart, its chambers
quiet and disturbed.
The air of new life
mingles with burial perfumes.
On the ground, limp wrappings
in long curls.
Thieves, I said.
Not the truth, not yet.

Even when he stood with me
I couldn't see.
Like dementia. A stranger
(was it the gardener?)
approaches as though he knows me.
Recognition is a blow finally,
and when I stand again
I rise slowly, as if balancing
on my shoulders two brimming
water jars that threaten to spill.

Like his skin
stung even by his own breaths
after death's flay.
My eyes open and close
until the impossible
has flickered into my body.

As at the visitation:
the face a parched desert
telling me to compose myself,
that it was true.
That I needed to get up,
go tell the men.

Death of a Minor Character Off-Stage

When you betray the hero,
It is not your own wish

But a stage command.
You're a puppet, mouthing

The words you're given to speak.
Subtle contexts are ignored.

The louder characters still shout
From the stage. You perform

Your duty, then abscond with the money.
Now, as night lowers around you,

Cut the threads that held you
In the narrative. Lean over

Your small fire as it dies.
Wait for the heroes to arrive.

The Incredible Shrinking Man

"They're all laughing at me, the incredible scientist."

That's Scott Carey talking. He's waiting for the anti-toxin
that never comes. The very diminished doctor is talking
with his normal-sized wife. He says, let's get out of here,
it's all too much. And you think maybe if they did go
somewhere alone it would all work out. Who cares
that he's shrinking. They could make it work.
But he does resent her, her size, or maybe just size
in general. The pillows, his notebooks, the sofas,
they're all huge, his world becoming larger than him.

After one night of domestic angst—"I felt puny and absurd.
I loathed myself"—he runs out into the evening air,
goes to the carnival and sees the sideshow, Tiny Tina
standing next to the Bearded Lady. After the show
he drinks coffee with her, and they hold cups
big as washbasins. He's happy at finding her,
her tiny hands, her perfect small face. But it's brief.
He shrinks past her as well. Eventually his wife
thinks he's been eaten by their cat, and the death
is announced over the evening news.

But maybe you know the movie and know he's not dead.
He's in the cellar with the huge matches and water drop,
the minor details now enormous, now his life.
He adapts quickly, lives in the box of matches,
drinks from the pool of the water drop. Still, he shrinks
past each new adjustment, all the time continuing to think
he can dominate each successively smaller world, first
fighting off the spiders, then the amoebas. He asks:
Does it mean less when you are the only one
experiencing something? Does it mean less
when there are so many who feel the same way?

He becomes an existentialist, which gives the movie
an oddly hopeful ending—he's alive. He knows
that as long as he knows he's alive, he's alive.
Even if he's smaller than a human cell.
Even if no one else can see him. It's light we see
at the end, and him looking up into it.

Host

It was a difficult worship.
Candles at the foot of each statue
marked exile. Like the white shirt
which enveloped my body in uniform.
Heat and cotton raised
an elementary sweat over how
I might damage Christ's body,
the thin wafer snapped into half moons
or a slower, agonized disintegration.

Through the drone of Mass
I considered Christ's exposure,
the arch of his torso opening
between shadowed bones.
Mary had eyes and a mouth.
The rest fell in folded marble robe.
A slight humor played on her lips.
Her only expression trailed
from a metal urn the priest swung,
spilled heavy incense
that perfumed the entire church.

What cannot be banished submerges
and returns slyly indirect.
Like dream, considering the self
as object, a chalice which the priest
drinks from, then wipes reverently clean
of his trace. Or the Host applied to tongue,
then swallowed by the body's dark.

After Mass, I'd linger by the votives
to watch the vows release,
watch the thin flames

eat through wax. It woke
my faith in the body, our beautiful
paradox: flesh made lucid
by the same light that devours it.

Confessional

First, its pleasures—
the still air like a glove.
Dim chamber lulling
the pupils wide, each small
sound chirring up to high ceiling.
The curtain's crushed velvet
hangs like faith congealed.
Behind it, he waits
while I kneel at a simple altar
and ironical window,
a thicker dark.

The slat between us
scrapes open. There is a grill
through which he speaks,
a blankness leaning close
to ask why I'm here.
We enter the ritual
of disclosure, pausing
at the fear between our words.
As my weak secrets trickle out,
he shifts, wanting more,
but holds in polite restraint.

I stall, the specifics
all seem interchangeable.
This appetite, that.
But what am I without my sins?
His ear is an insect trap
drawing them into a jar
where they crawl over one another,

revealed. Then I am blessed
and step outside, expecting
to be healed. But all I feel is the lingering
drone of his thieving voice,
its velvet drop and echo.

Accident

It's too much
like love
for me not to shudder
as I drive by, though no one
in this instance is dead
or even badly injured.
Fumes from spilled gasoline
filter into the cab
and at once intoxicate
and clarify my sense.

A young man,
a boy really,
sits dazed on a curb.
The blow has just fallen
and won't resurface
for some time.
He says everything is okay,
everything is fine
and repeats these words
until they're an even breathing.

Fibrillation
will come later,
the nervous jumps that counter
his present slowness.
Now, the sky is blue.
He sits on the curb. It's hard.
The cement scrapes his hand,
burns.

He's separated from his vehicle
and sits quietly,

a stunned mouse
after the cat didn't kill him.
Perhaps, with me, he is considering
the beauty of police cars—
black, white, the red throb on top.
But they are style at a bad time.
The star
is pretty on a shirt.
The badge a silver raft
on deep blue. So the questions
shock, the insistence on knowing
what happened. They want answers.

It could still explode,
the gasoline ignite from a casual aside
dropped like the cigarette
of a passerby. The explosion
would send a shudder
through my distant car
and two or three lives
would lift on the heat,
bright orange fanning through
and out.

Bent July Landscape

A cicada's clumsy flight
into the side of my face,
its crude husk the source
of that spilled, obsessive sound.
It is beautiful as it leaves,
flying down the hill
away from sight.
The stunted cherry and green plum
root into the disturbed fields
with thistle and cheatgrass,
their mute past given now to hardness,
to the small fruits they make,
like my own heavy limbs, flightless.
They take their disfigurement quietly.
A mockingbird breaks into a royal anne,
flies off with a piece of white flesh.

The Woman Who Fell from the Observation Deck of the Empire State Building Confesses

That first sentence was the only true one—
forgive me, Father, for I have sinned.
All I ever told were lies.
And when those lines left my lips
I felt breathless,
but afterwards smiled for days.
Is that why I'm here now?
No. I'm finally ready to tell the truth.
I agreed with you the whole time.
Death is worth dressing up for.
But I was afraid, Father, and I felt it
the minute I walked into church.
Rule number one,
never relax in church.
You seem to know this,
you're so heavy with people
and their other lives—
you sit that way.
This is how I went:
gloves, a skirt,
I put on lipstick,
my best pumps, silk stockings,
and climb 86 floors, all of them.
I come for the fall, not the view.
The sky is white.
Then I'm past the rail
and I'm absolutely right. The fall
is baptism, my body wet
and opening. It removes my shoes
and then the stockings, takes my breath.
I see how beautiful it is,

each a still-frame,
a movie reflected
until the car hood
and then I'm barefoot
asleep on a Buick.

Father Madigan

The Latin incantations
have become my breathing,
but only because I take little
meaning from words. In Mass
I watch the candle flames
quiver when the choir sings.
Voice can crack a thing.
I used to think I felt
God run through me
to the Host and chalice,
but that was my own
burning I fed them.

I try to contain their distortions,
but they escape like heat.
We have little choice.
I know that; they don't want to.
And I know what to do,
the penance—I say them,
they do them and then walk out
into the gray matter of no choice.

I picture sin as a seagull.
It lands where it wants,
its yellow eye anchored on the senses.

PRESTO, CHANGE-O!

Prosaic Opening

The prosaic opening of the blossoms
in morning. First breath after breath
has been held, a thousand sharp intakes,
then exhale and a gloss of pollen sugars the air.

Or an eye. Heart heavy on its bent stem,
but the head rolls back to take the sun's weight,
its indifferent magnitudes. One reflexive blink
as the aperture dilates to what it can admit.

Or a door. Some putz standing in the desert
for years before his Egyptian riddle until
thick stone gates roll away like the ocean parting
for his stroll down the middle when he stumbles
onto the right word, mutters it softly in his sleep.

Lantern

In the morning damp,
I light the carved pumpkin
through its eye,
tilt the lid up and find a snail
hanging underneath, a glistening
black line.

It siphons into the fresh
cavern, past heat-smoothed thread
until the flame builds,
becomes unbearable,
and it slides back
into the curve
of its shell and falls.

As I blow out the candle,
I toss the snail to the ground
and light another match
to watch the fire through wood,
the char and curl.

My grandfather smoking,
I remember him slowly lighting
cigarettes with a shaking hand,
disease claiming his body
as the body abandoned him.
He'd lift the match up
and almost light himself.

Oracle Bone

It was most often the lower carapace
of a turtle shell. Sometimes an ox scapula.
The bone was sanded and grooved,
then the Court Diviners shouted
their question at the Dead.
The reply was recorded with a flaming stick
pressed to bone, a series of sharp cracks
as the notches were seared.
They picked out characters
from the tangled fracture and read the prophesy.
Then the bones were neatly stored.

That was 3,000 years ago: China, Shang Dynasty.
One more dead art form.
Now, a crack team of scientists
scavenge them for clues to what we were.

But we can know it in our own bones.
The literal is easiest—a clean break
traced on X-ray and an ache to go with it
year after year. Even hairline fracture
is a distinct thread through humerus.
The obscure demands blind faith
and a backbone of patience
climbed year after year.

The ilium's pelvic cove
curves in us like the moon.
Now we've walked on that giant face.
What believer ages ago was certain
we'd add our footprints
to the tracery on her skin?
Small and miles away,

she still rises every night
and tells a different quarter of her story,
the same truth she always tells:
years orbiting the parent,
then slow apprehension
of a more distant, enormous sun.

If I could slip a bone from its sleeve,
I'd learn to read my own scars,
crosses and stars the language of fire,
a text that will be stored
with all the others.
Flesh is a temporary confusion,
a chance to consider what lasts.
Blood flares—then dries,
leaving a pile of scorched bones
to tell how love burned through us.
One more dead art form.

When others excavate our hieroglyphs,
We'll be locked into the next puzzle.
And they'll find what we found:

We contain the answer to every question

The Dead will help us

Our marrow is a medium
through which God sings

Wasted Prayer

That bird shit might smite him on the head.

That I would have dinner with the great dead writers.

That the train would reach Philadelphia in the next half hour.

That I meet Muhammad Ali.

That the man I love would love me back.

That God is merciful to all the dead celebrities.

That I use more than 3% of my brain.

Escaping My Death Again

For Harry Houdini

My advice: Imagine
every variable.
Anticipate how it might go awry.
Be willing to break any bone you have to.

I was most in danger when I failed
to anticipate the smallest detail: The effect
of cold on metal. The day's weather.
How the current ran.

It's when I've seen him
smiling from the bridge, disguised
in street clothes, standing with the others.
The gleam in his eye unmistakable. Such happiness

he would take at my failure, that was clear.
He'd love to collect my bones
for his side show. Tack up my skin
under glass. He'd save the headlines,
the yellowing picture of a shocked crowd.
They'd take up a corner of a back room
until he got bored,
and then I'd be in storage or on sale.

It's actually good
to catch that glance
just before you slip
through water. It can save
your life, like the thin layer of air
between ice and river.
Because you won't let that jackal
take you, not this time.

Because that sliding smile
springs my escape. And then I'm guided
shoulders first through a hole in ice,
lifted to the boat, water and steam
streaming from me,
a blanket quickly thrown around
my shoulders.

Octopus Trick

as seen on Jacques Cousteau's *Silent World*

He fills the container, arms crammed
against the curved glass wall,
the way he lives in his own elastic skin.
Eyes like olives in a martini
dryly survey as the rest of him
feels out the escape route
at the jar's neck. The hole
only needs to be a degree larger
than the beak. He eases through
an eye-hole's diameter,
slipping to deck like a newborn,
then slides and muscles to ship's edge
for the drop back into water,
which happens in a quick mess.
A spill into ocean, then he's invisible
and lost, a pale star falling
the dark way down to bottom.

Sounding

Surrounded by crowd, that nightmare
sound, you filled my ear
with hundreds of words,
each landing like a feather.
Your eyes were veiled, mouth held
still as possible, the careful stance
of nonchalance. As though you didn't
care who was there, whose ear
you slurred into, whose eyes
you avoided. But your murmur
was more than words slung one
after the other, more than a low
level tone clinically detailing
your past life and nightmares, and how
you got through. I could graph
the timber, pitch, and control,
and it might approximate the abstract
your voice became, a song, really,
like the sirens sing. But your immaculate
distant shore fronts a wild, and even you
don't know where the call comes from,
which nightmare, or which past life.
Or why it insinuates above the clatter
of silverware against wine glasses
and through the endless chatter,
the drone louder, then subdued
as the heads turn above their plates.
Why your voice, low and sliding
like water under sand, should intrude
through the noise, fill my glass,
the one I just drank from,
still quaking with sound
after I put it down on the table.

Great Waters of the Eastern Coast

The men ride their motor's sputter
against the water, tapping out a weakness—
theirs. The ocean is fine, always fine.
It never needed what they're after,
their fierceness a drunken excess.

Like the man in the bar the night before
who prodded the bouncer with a warped pool cue
and the next moment was on the floor,
hands over his head, begging for mercy.

Mercy. The shrinking houses on shore
are dice. The men look away from them.
The sea's wide pull
demands their full attention.
The hands toughen on rope,
pulling to feel something.

As they return, the town overwhelms
with size, each house growing
until it's more than a remote idea
to keep someone happy on the water.
The boats straggle home and wait
in line. The men come back
through the streets, reeking of fish
and engine oil, their catch
still alive in the hold.

That man had to get up,
rock to his feet and harangue
the doorman again, had to get thrown out,
jacket after him, too drunk
to feel the street he fell on.

Sanctum

I make myself watch
as the organs are removed,
rinsed and poured into jars
looking like peach halves or rhubarb.

The canopic heads delight me:
grinning, stern, mild and merciless.
I wore them so well!
I love theater even now.

But when the heart is sealed
in its separate chamber,
ache vibrates
where it used to dwell and I can't
hide anymore. How unfair.

Now relatives gather
around my body's clean hearth,
reminisce how at birth I was
put together and held in warm arms,
a welcome as odd as this party.

Gold leaf presses my eyelids closed.
I've feared blindness
the way others don't want to know.
Now I flee to more foreign senses,
try to distinguish the perfumes filling me.
Resin, honey, natron,
and that leveling scent
cutting through them all.

My arms are wrapped
and folded with linens that fit

like a uterine glove,
pleasing my love for symmetry.
The thin crust of symbols
hooked to my embittered shell
serve me well:
The thick bronze face covers my transparency;
A jade scarab will resurrect my heart's waste;
An ivory eye over the forehead
signals my neglected gift.
I must navigate with it now.

Symbols are sanctum
I understand as I'm lowered
into the first coffin, a safe room
to sit with my grim analyst,
Conciliatory, but I'm disarmed.
No more Mr. Charm.

As the second coffin quakes shut,
my nostalgia seeps with the myrrh.
If I still had a marrow, it would glow
with cheap emotion. But I'm hollow
and bound, an oiled skin
pushed through reeds
onto water. Even now I fight surrender,
the wrong fight, I understand
only as the waters part
around me in welcome.

Duck Pickers

Under the basement's single bulb
they pick, backs curved over, eyes down
so that you look for rosaries,
and then the heads, swinging dead weights,
are no surprise.

Except for those blood-heavy,
feathers fall
as though passing through water.
This part is easy,
the ducks stripped to the shoulders,
the head and neck left covered,
made absurd. They worry out
pinfeathers, then drop the mallard
or widgeon or teal onto the rounding pile
to their side. The bodies
hold together, hoarding black
between them.

When the picking is finished,
the wings become fans
separated into their own pile, and the heads
become heads, tongues extended,
bead eyes gone smoke.

They open the ducks,
gut them first, counting the organs,
or scald them in boiling water
to wet small feathers
fingers otherwise can't isolate.
The singeing is last,

the fine hair small flares
as flame reaches skin.

They know this smell
that stays,
take it into their hands
with heat from the matches.

One Day in the Whale

Acapunth. Mimsrur. Jonah tries out the words
this new place compels him to say. The sound
hums through his colon, then liver, a deep tremor,
and he would cry as he speaks back
but there is only room for the slow torsion
of tongue, teeth and lip.

Wolzforge. he has no idea what it means
but the literal doesn't worry him
the way it used to, since he might not be alive.
This, right here, is exactly what he thought death was,
cramping and more cramping and without light.
He seems to be in the middle of it.

His right leg aches in spasm, but he's letting go
of what he knew, like "leg" and "ache."
He's getting good at letting go. From when
he confessed and almost enjoyed the throw overboard;
definitely he did appreciate going under,
that instant cap of silence and slow fall
to stillness. Lungs blooming with carbon
until they couldn't answer, and he had met
everything he most feared.

Xanthen. The ocean you can disappear into.
His closed eyelids press against hard peritoneum.
He can't be sure it's his own flexing.
His nerves are reaching past memory.
Mimoleth. Shimnel. They are his miraculous
transition, his secret boat
which he mistakes for death.

Gogol, Toward St. Petersburg

I remember pushing that cat under
with a stick. It bobbed from the pond,
a slick anima, and I pushed it down
again and again until I felt it die.

In summers, the wheat hoarded its quiet
as though dead, and heat spread
across the pond's smooth skin.

Toward St. Petersburg in winter
the white plains gave way to each other
and in the village with its smell of tar
the horses shook when we stopped.

I never grew accustomed to the clatter
of people, the distortion of Vasilyevka's church,
but my mother's words unburied
the cat and I never did get it back under.
Instead, it wavered in me, a pale voice
between heaven and hell.

When I burned dead souls, I laid them out
page by page for the flames
and the fire took me with it,
the rim of ash my unpurifiable body,
its white heart.

Unmaking the Horse

You approach its form
of mud. Close, you notice
twigs mixed in,
the odd gill of its bent neck
cool breath escapes through.

Tendrils of oxygen
refuse to leave its muzzle,
and you hear earth compressing,
unsettling.

Its ears sawed to shells,
eyes folded in
with shock.

It is strangely silent
as it lies down.
First to its knees and then
a black moon before you.

Finally, beauty is sent back
through the long funnel
to abstraction

and you are left
with its bare remains,
broken landscape,
your own breath, taking.

Afterlife

for May Wirth

The woman rides a white horse.

The horse canters steadily around the ring,
a given in the equations they make.

When she back-flips off the horse's crescent rump,
she and the horse know she will always return.

From the side, perhaps, to a handstand
or to splits, then one leg across the horse's withers,

hanging to skim the circle's edge.
The woman is drunk with the circles they travel,

and when she somersaults, at the height of the spin,
seconds dilate, and she stays suspended,

apprehending her arc, the arch of that horse's
white neck, and the ring enclosing them.

The lights turn the rosined back and her hands
orange. She holds them up, two lit gloves.

They have always been this color.

Fortunetelling Fish

When they slide out of the net
back into the water,
the ocean is out for you.
And when a fin cuts your flesh,
you will die young.

What you want is for bellies
to flash on the decks
like silver.

If the eyes come out
in your palm, you will die
of strangulation.
If the colors in the scales fade,
you will lose the ability to dream
and your sleep will become
a useless cave.
If the belly breaks open
and a deer antler falls out,
your bones will cripple you.

When you finish,
hose the decks off.
Any blood left on the wood
will seek you out,
enter you, then mark
your skin and everyone
will see the stain.

You want the fish to ripple
peacefully into barrels,
no spilling.

If your hand passes through one
to the other side,

then that's a sign
your mind will fail
so gradually you won't recognize
your face in glass
and will turn away

loved ones as strangers.
Do not step on a fish
or the right side of your body
will fall into loose net.

And after you've run your hands
smoothly across their bodies,
then stretch your arms to the sun,
you will forget fish,
forget family, the past,
your loves,
even your name.

Every letter,
every sound.